TO

FROM

DATE

The NATURE OF SUCCESS

MAC ANDERSON
BY THE FOUNDER OF *Successories*®

COUNTRYMAN

Nashville, Tennessee

Copyright © 2003 by Mac Anderson

Published by J. Countryman®, a division of Thomas Nelson, Inc.,
Nashville, Tennessee 37214

Unless otherwise noted, all Scripture quotations used in this book are from the
New King James Version of the Bible ©1979, 1980, 1982, 1992, Thomas
Nelson, Inc., Publisher.

The New International Version of the Bible (NIV) © 1984 by the International
Bible Society. Used by permission of Zondervan Bible Publishers.

Project Editor: Kathy Baker

Design: Koechel Peterson and Associates, Inc., Mpls, MN

ISBN 1–4041–0011–3

Printed and bound in Belgium

www.thomasnelson.com
www.jcountryman.com

table of contents

FOLLOW YOUR

SUCCESS IS A JOURNEY,

NOT A DESTINATION.

DREAMS

Successful is the person who has lived well, laughed often, and loved much, who has never lacked appreciation for the earth's beauty, who never fails to look for the best in others or give the best of themselves.

IT WAS A MOMENT I'll never forget. I had just finished speaking to a group, and the president of the company gave me one of the greatest compliments I had ever received. He said, "Never stop what you're doing, for you are blessed with the ability to connect with people . . . soul to soul."

Put simply, that is my goal for this book—to connect with your soul—because one idea, if it's the right one, can change your life. Over the past thirty years, I've been very blessed to have been involved in three successful start-up companies, and in *The Nature of Success*, I'm sharing with you many of the lessons I've learned about business and life.

Because I strongly believe that people remember great stories long after we'll forget great lectures, my "lessons learned" are told mostly through real-life stories to share my twenty-eight keys to success.

Success is a very personal thing, but I think most people would agree that true success is about being fulfilled in life. It's that feeling of deep satisfaction that starts in your soul and radiates through your being. The end result is true happiness and peace of mind. I would think that there is no greater feeling than to look back toward the end of your life with a "smile in your heart," knowing that many of your dreams came true, and that you made a positive difference in the lives of others.

It is my sincere hope that this book will be a useful and practical tool to help you:

- Discover your personal definition of success
- Discover your core existence, or your reason for being
- Set clearly defined goals
- Never waiver in your belief that you can achieve them
- Manage your attitude
- Persevere when adversity strikes . . . and it will
- Learn to take risks and embrace change
- Keep kindness in your heart . . . always
- Love and be loved
- Make a difference whenever, wherever, and however, you can.

Yes, life truly is a journey, and here's wishing you the very best on yours.

MAC ANDERSON

BEHIND ME IS INFINITE POWER,

BEFORE ME IS ENDLESS POSSIBILITY,

AROUND ME IS BOUNDLESS OPPORTUNITY.

WHY SHOULD I FEAR?

BELIEF

DISCOVER THE POWER
of Belief

FOR MORE THAN *one hundred years, runners tried to break the four–minute mile. It was considered the "Holy Grail" of track and field. Many said it couldn't be done. In fact, doctors wrote articles in medical journals explaining why it was physically impossible for the human body to run a mile in less than four minutes.*

However, in May 1954, a British medical student named Roger Bannister ran the mile in 3:59.4. His amazing accomplishment made headlines around the world. Yet what happened afterward is even more amazing. The four-minute mile was broken again the next month…and then again…and again. It has since been broken than 700 times, sometimes by several people in the same race.

What happened? They weren't training any differently, but for the first time they believed they could do it. The barriers to the mind had come down.

Never underestimate the power of belief when it comes to fulfilling your dreams. I can say with no hesitation that every person I've ever met who has achieved any degree of success has had one thing in common: they believed with all their heart they could do it.

Early in my career, I was the vice president of sales for a food company. One time I was in Detroit hiring a sales person for the market. We had lined up eight appointments for the day, and the morning had been a bust.

I looked up and my 1 o'clock appointment was standing at the door. He was a tall, good–looking guy, and I remember thinking, "This could be the one." We talked for about fifteen minutes, and I asked a question I always ask, "What will you be doing five years from now?" I'll never forget his answer. He said, "Mr. Anderson, the way these appointments have been going, I might still be interviewing!" Well, that wasn't exactly what I wanted to hear. We talked for a few more minutes and I excused him.

Then I looked up and my 2 o'clock was there. He walked over and gave me a confident handshake, and a few minutes later I asked the same question, "What are you going to be doing five years from now?" He looked me right in the eye and said, "Mr. Anderson, I'm going to be working for you. This job fills my skills and my needs to a tee. I don't just think, I know I can sell your product in this market. And furthermore, if you don't like my performance after thirty days, you don't owe me a cent."

Well, you could have knocked me over with a feather! He had just made me an offer I couldn't refuse. But the offer had nothing to do with the money I might save; it had everything to do with his unwavering passion and belief he could do it. Within a year, Sam was the number one sales person in the company.

You see, whether you think you can, or think you can't . . . you're right!

The only thing that stands between a person and what they want in life is the will to try it and the faith to believe it possible.

RICH DEVOS

NOTHING GREAT WAS EVER ACHIEVED
WITHOUT ENTHUSIASM.

RALPH WALDO EMERSON

ENTHUSIASM

Belief Fuels ENTHUSIASM

IN 1972 I HAD JUST *accepted a position as vice president of sales for Orval Kent Food Company, a small enterprise that manufactured fresh–prepared salad products selling to delicatessens and restaurants. I had come on board to hire and train new sales people, but I knew absolutely nothing about the salad business. So Sid Caisman, who had spent most of his career selling to delicatessens, was assigned to show me the ropes. Sid was a pro, and he loved what he did.*

I'd been there about two weeks when Sid came in smiling ear to ear. He said, "Mac, I've been trying to get an appointment with this large grocery chain for over two years and I finally have it next Friday. Do you want to go with me?" My response: "You bet I do!"

17

The big day arrived, and on our way out we picked up our refrigerated samples. When we arrived at their corporate headquarters I could tell Sid was pumped. The buyer came out and introduced himself, and we followed him back to his office. We sat down and he looked across his desk at Sid and asked, "What makes you think your product is any better than your competitors'?"

That was Sid's cue to perform. He began to tell the buyer about why our potato salad was superior to anything on the market. He went into great detail about the quality, the fresh–diced vegetables, our special dressing and our state of the art manufacturing plant. Then he said, "And I've saved the best for last . . . you're going to love how it tastes!"

With great fanfare, Sid popped open the lid of the sample container, and I couldn't believe it. Sitting right on top was a large, black, rotten potato about the size of a quarter. But Sid, seeing the potato before the buyer did, reached down and popped it in his mouth and said, "Bob, I just can't get enough of this stuff!" And to my surprise the buyer also reached down, grabbed some salad, and said, "Sid, you're right. It tastes great."

It was a powerful moment. I had just witnessed a sophisticated buyer eating potato salad with his fingers and he didn't even know it! And it was all for one reason . . . Sid's unbridled enthusiasm.

Many things will catch your eye,
but only a few will catch your heart...
pursue those.

ENTHUSIASM

PASSION

THE WAVE OF PASSION
CAN BECOME
AN UNSTOPPABLE FORCE.

Ride the Wave
OF PASSION

WHAT HAPPENS WHEN *you believe something with all your heart? Belief fuels enthusiasm, and determined enthusiasm explodes into passion. It fires our souls and lifts our spirits.*

In 1991, when Successories® hired Tim Dumbler as a corporate account manager, he shared his goal of becoming number one in the company with his manager, Neil Sexton. But Neil, quite frankly, had serious doubts that Tim could make it through the first month, much less be number one.

Neil's first two interviews with Tim were conducted over the phone, and he passed those with flying colors. But when Neil met Tim for the first time, he was shocked when Tim told him he was legally blind. He began to lose his sight when he was in the third grade from a rare disease called macular degeneration. Tim acknowledged he would have problems entering orders into the computers, but he had a possible solution. He told Neil about a machine that he could hook up to magnify the letters on the screen to two inches high. Tim was willing to buy it if he could have the job.

After the conversation, Neil came to my office and explained the situation. I said, "Neil, let's give him a chance," but I must admit, I had serious doubts that Tim could do it.

Well, we were dead wrong. We grossly underestimated Tim's passion and his determination to succeed. Even though it took him much longer to enter the orders, Tim made it work. He came in early. He worked late. Whatever it took, he did it.

In 1991, Tim's first year, he was tops of ten experienced corporate sales reps, with over $500,000 in sales. In 1994 he was number one again with $700,000, and again in 1997 with $950,000. His customers loved him because when you can't see, you become a great listener. His peers loved him because of his caring, positive attitude.

He was certainly an inspiration to me, too. I asked him one time, "Tim, how do you stay so positive?" He said, "Mac, it's unfortunate that I'm visually impaired, but I have to tell you that fighting through the adversity has made me a better person. I have come to realize that I *have* a lot more than I don't have. I love my family, I love my work and the people I work with. I've been blessed in many ways."

Tim's passion has propelled him to great successes.

DARE TO SOAR

BUT THOSE WHO WAIT ON THE LORD SHALL RENEW

THEIR STRENGTH; THEY SHALL MOUNT UP WITH WINGS

LIKE EAGLES, THEY SHALL RUN AND NOT BE WEARY,

THEY SHALL WALK AND NOT FAINT.

ISAIAH 40:31

Manage Your ATTITUDE

AFTER MORE THAN THIRTY YEARS *in business, I'm convinced that the difference in success and failure is not how you look, not how you dress, not how you're educated . . . but how you think.*

It's impossible for me to overstate the importance of maintaining a positive attitude. On the other hand, it's impossible to understate the difficulty in actually doing it. Staying positive is not easy, and it's a very personal thing. But it can be done. I can only share what works for me and hope that you can relate to my experience.

First on my list is exercise. Without question my levels of motivation and energy are tied to exercise. Have you seen those long strands of Christmas lights with about one hundred little white lights on each strand? What happens when one of those bulbs becomes loose? They all go out. They shut down. That's what happens to me when I don't exercise. It's my top "stress buster."

Second on my list if to live with gratitude. William James, one of the fathers of modern psychology, said, "The greatest discovery of my generation is that a human being can alter their life by altering their attitude." Abraham Lincoln said, "People are as happy as they make up their minds to be."

We are blessed in so many ways, and we need to remind ourselves continually of those blessings. When we wake up each morning, we have choices to make: We can choose our socks, choose our underwear, and most importantly, we choose our attitudes.

The third key for me to manage my attitude is to laugh at myself and laugh with others. Many people take themselves far too seriously. As kids we laugh a lot, we dream a lot, but then we grow up and we become a heart attack waiting to happen!

Researchers have investigated why some people can't cope and found three reasons:

- Low self–esteem
- Living in the past
- Can't laugh at themselves

In fact, one study indicates that we need a minimum of twelve laughs a day just to stay healthy. Laugh at yourself! Laugh with your friends, your family, your co–workers. It will keep you going, keep you healthy, and keep you motivated.

PURPOSE

MAY IT BE SAID,
WHEN THE SUN SETS ON YOUR LIFE,
YOU MADE A DIFFERENCE.

DISCOVER YOUR
Reason for Being

*The creation
of a thousand forests
is in one acorn.*

RALPH WALDO EMERSON

WHAT ARE YOUR *greatest gifts? How can you best serve mankind? These are questions you must answer to find your true purpose in life.*

Who am I?

What am I meant to do here?

What am I trying to do with my life?

These are powerful questions that can be difficult to answer. They sometimes surface during major life transitions such as family strife, job loss, spiritual awakenings, or the death of a loved one.

I feel fortunate to have found my purpose in life. I have that reason to get up in the morning and it fuels my passion. In one of the greatest compliments I ever received, someone said to me, "Mac, when you speak you've been blessed with the ability to connect with others . . . soul to soul." I thought about those words and have chosen to shape my life around that gift. My purpose through speaking and writing is to "bring ideas to life" that will encourage and motivate people.

Every person is a unique being. There is only one of you in the universe. You have many obvious gifts and other gifts still waiting to be discovered.

I truly believe, however, that one of the most important questions you can ask yourself in your journey to find your purpose is, "How can I serve others?" Albert Schweitzer said it well: "I don't know what your destiny will be, but one thing I do know: the only ones among you who will be really happy are those who have sought and found how to serve."

KNOWLEDGE

KNOWLEDGE IS LIKE CLIMBING A MOUNTAIN;

THE HIGHER YOU REACH

THE MORE YOU CAN SEE AND APPRECIATE

DEVELOP AN UNQUENCHABLE
Thirst for Knowledge

*Human power
and human
knowledge
meet in one.*

FRANCIS BACON

NOT TOO LONG AGO, *I had the opportunity to hear Jim Cathcart speak to a corporate audience. Jim is a good friend, and a great speaker. He told the story of how listening to a radio program over twenty-five years ago changed his life forever, and with his permission I'd like to share it with you.*

In 1972, he was working at the Little Rock, Arkansas Housing Authority, making $525 a month, with a new wife and baby at home, no college degree, no past successes, and not much hope for the foreseeable future.

One morning, he was sitting in his office listening to the radio, to a program called "*Our Changing World*" by Earl Nightingale, who was known as "the Dean of Personal Motivation." That day, Nightingale, in his booming voice, said something that would change Jim's life forever: "If you will spend an extra hour each day in study of your chosen field, you will be a national expert in that field in five years or less."

Jim was stunned, but the more he thought about it the more it made sense. Although he had never given a speech, he had always wanted to help people grow in areas of personal development and motivation. He began his quest to put Nightingale's theory to the test by reading books and listening to tapes whenever he could. He also started exercising, became better organized, and joined a self-improvement study group. He persisted through weeks of temptations to quit, just by doing a little more each day to further his goal. Within six months he had learned more than he had in his few years of college, and he began to believe he could turn his goal of becoming a motivational speaker into reality. All the hard work, the discipline, and study paid off. Jim now has delivered more than 2,500 speeches worldwide and has won every major award in the speaking industry.

Just like companies have market value, so do people. In the simplest terms, your market value increases by knowing and doing more. Knowledge is power, not only for your career, but also to improve your family and spiritual life. I once heard a quote that sums it up well, "Knowledge is like climbing a mountain; the higher you reach the more you can see and appreciate."

PROGRESS

INCH BY INCH
LIFE'S A CINCH.
YARD BY YARD
LIFE IS HARD.

SET REALISTIC *Short-term* GOALS

WHEN I WAS A FRESHMAN *in college I learned an unforgettable lesson.*

I was having a rough week when there was a lot to do and very little time to do it. I was overwhelmed. I panicked.

That night a friend stopped by my dorm room. When I told him my problem, he said, "Mac, I'll share something with you that my grandmother told me a few years ago. She said to always remember: 'Inch by inch, life's a cinch. Yard by yard, life is hard.'"

I said, "Bob, come on. Here I am drowning in work and your lifeline is a quote from your grandmother."

After he left, however, those twelve little words kept dancing in my head. I took out a piece of notebook paper and listed all the things I had to do in the next three days. That night I began knocking them off one by one.

Three days later I took out that paper and marked through the last thing on the list. It felt great! And then I took out another piece of paper and wrote down the words: "Inch by inch, life's a cinch. Yard by yard, life is hard." I then folded the paper and put it in my wallet. As many of you know, I've been collecting quotes ever since.

You see, success doesn't come cascading like Niagara Falls; it comes one drop at a time through short–term, realistic goals.

Experts on motivation disagree on a lot of things, but one thing they all agree on is that your levels of motivation are directly tied to your expected probabilities of success. In other words, if you believe you can do something (the goals are realistic), you're likely to be highly motivated. If, however, you think you can't (because the goals are unrealistic) your motivation level falls greatly.

The lesson here is to continue to dream big dreams, but realize that the short–term goals that take you to the next plateau are the real keys to success.

Goals
are dreams
with deadlines.

PROGRESS

IMAGINE

TAP YOUR *Creative Soul*

IMAGINATION IS SEEING *things, not as they are, but as they could be. Think about it: Everything that has ever been invented in the history of the world began as an idea in one person's mind. Without imagination, without dreams, we would stay fixed in time.*

Many people have asked me how I started Successories®. They've asked, "Did you wake up in the middle of the night and say, 'Aha! Combining motivational words with beautiful photographs would be a great way to reinforce corporate values and personal goals'?" Didn't happen! What did happen is

41

the way most great ideas come to life—it evolved. It started with my love of quotations. I've always felt that the right quote can bring an idea to life. It's like looking through a camera and seeing a fuzzy image that with one twitch of the lens becomes crystal clear.

The love of quotes inspired me to compile my favorites in a small 80–page book titled *Motivational Quotes* in 1985. The book was first used as a corporate gift, but then we decided to offer it as an item in airport gift shops. Much to our surprise, we sold more than 800,000 copies in the next two years. Along the way, however, we added an order form encouraging the reader to select their favorite quote in the book, and for $19.95 we would ship it to them on a brass plaque. Much to our delight, the phones ran off the hook.

The Big Idea for Successories® was on the verge of being born. We had discovered that many people loved quotes as much as I did. We went from motivational quote books, to brass quote plaques, to motivational wall décor, which would combine breathtaking photography with inspirational words. A simple idea, but I've learned that many times the simple ideas are the best ideas.

But good ideas don't just happen. They depend on people who are open to making them happen, people who are eager to explore new paths and have a burning desire to learn new things. Jordan Ayan, an expert on creativity, says in his book *Ignite Your Creative Spark* that new ideas have roots in your creative soul, and a four-step process will help you bring them to life.

The four steps are:

1. Preparation—You gather information and resources to fully understand a problem or opportunity.

2. Incubation—You take no conscious action toward solving your problem; instead you just let your subconscious mind play with the information.

3. Illumination—You experience the "Aha" moment, probably when you are least expecting it.

4. Implementation—You do . . . or you don't. This is where most people fall off the creative train. I heard John Maxwell once say, "Lots of folks have great ideas in the shower, but they seem to lose them when they dry off." Don't be one of those people. Use persistence and passion to bring your ideas to life.

Nothing happens…
but first a dream.
CARL SANDBURG

CHANGE

SOMETIMES IN THE WINDS

OF CHANGE WE FIND

OUR TRUE DIRECTION.

Embrace CHANGE IN YOUR LIFE

THE ROOT WORD *for "motivation" is "move," and movement is change. Ask yourself right now … Am I moving forward, or am I standing still? Do I have a career that I love? Am I pleased with the relationship I have with my spouse, my kids? Do I have a healthy lifestyle? Is my energy level, my attitude, where it should be? Is my relationship with God where it should be? Is there a hobby, an activity I've wanted to pursue?*

Truthful answers to these and other questions will tell you whether you *want*, or *need* to change.

Although answering such questions truthfully is critical to begin the change process, we all know the tough part comes later. According to John Murphy in his book *Think Change*, the key to successful change is discipline and "reprogramming beliefs." A cautionary inner voice will tell you not to rock the boat, to stay on the path of least resistance, but your heart is telling you otherwise.

Listen to your heart. Filter out the old static and tune in something new. Challenge your assumptions, identify and study people already doing what you want to do. Read books and listen to tapes that will motivate you to break away from the notorious "comfort zone." Confront your fears. When one unsatisfying day just blurs into the next—your life is begging for a change.

Comfort zones put padlocks on the doors to growth, discovery, and adventure in your life, but three keys that will unlock those doors are discipline, hard work, and faith. I'll repeat what I shared in Chapter 7. When it comes to progress, when it comes to change . . . *Inch by inch, life's a cinch. Yard by yard, life is hard.* Unlock one door at a time, enjoy small successes, and soon you will have achieved your goals.

Some key points to remember:

1. No pain! No gain! There will be some setbacks.

2. Fear is a human emotion. The absence of fear is not courage, it's brain damage.

3. Give your fear a name and it becomes a problem. It's easier to solve problems than conquer fear.

4. With each obstacle you overcome, your confidence will grow. Every time you conquer any fear . . . no matter how small . . . you are better prepared for the next challenge.

Change can truly be a wonderful gift. It can recharge your emotional battery and nourish your soul. Just do it! Choose change and let it make a positive difference in your life.

Change is inevitable. Growth is optional.

COURAGE

HEROES ARE ORDINARY PEOPLE
WHO PLACE THEIR DREAMS
ABOVE THEIR FEARS.

HAVE *Heroes*

LIFE CAN BE DIFFICULT. *Things don't always go as planned. Finding inspiration during these times can get us back on track. Sometimes just one thought can provide the energy and courage to fight through adversity. For me, at times, this courage comes from thinking of my personal heroes—people who accomplished great things under difficult circumstances, people who put their dreams above their fears . . . and won.*

Four heroes inspire me every time I think of them. Three you'll know, and one you won't.

The first is Mother Teresa, who devoted her life to caring for the poorest of the poor. Second, Helen Keller had every excuse to give up on life, yet she persevered and became an inspiration to millions. The third is Abraham Lincoln, who failed in two businesses and lost six elections before becoming the greatest president of the United States.

*Keep your face
to the sunshine,
and you will not see
the shadows*

HELEN KELLER

My fourth hero is Ricky Johnson. I only met him once, back when I was a sophomore in college, but I'll never forget him.

Nothing had gone right that hot summer day in Indiana. I was selling dictionaries door–to–door, and by 11 that morning, I still hadn't sold a book, I'd gotten two people out of bed, and I'd just been bitten by a German shepherd. Not a good day!

I dejectedly knocked on the door of a large frame house and was surprised to be greeted by a big smile and an invitation to enter. After Mrs. Johnson and I chatted for a minute or so, I began showing her the book. As I gave the presentation, she would say, "I'll bet Ricky would like that feature" or "Ricky was just asking me about that word."

Soon she said, "Let's go see what Ricky thinks." I followed her back to a small room, where I saw a 13–year–old boy lying in bed.

His legs were withered from polio. He looked through the dictionary and said, "Mom, I know this will help me with my school work." Then he asked me if I'd sold many books and where I went to college.

We talked for a few minutes, and then with eyes that were sparkling and a smile I will never forget, he said, "You know, Mac, I've never met anyone I didn't like. I like my teachers and my classmates. . . . They're so good to me. They even made me a special ramp to help me get up and down the steps." His last words as I left were, "Mac, someday I'm going to college just like you—I'll guarantee it."

I drove away from Ricky's house with a lump in my throat, a tear in my eye, and a warm, wonderful feeling inside, and I went on to have my best sales day of the summer. It had taken a 13-year-old boy to make me quit feeling sorry for myself—and I've never forgotten his wonderful attitude about life.

So often we worry about what we don't have and don't spend enough time being thankful for what we do have. Most of us are very blessed, but sometimes it takes a hero to remind us.

SOLITUDE

TRUE SILENCE IS THE REST OF THE MIND,
AND IT IS TO THE SPIRIT
WHAT SLEEP IS TO THE BODY—
NOURISHMENT AND REFRESHMENT.

WILLIAM PENN

Seek SOLITUDE

EVER NEED YOUR *emotional battery recharged? I know that when it's been too long since I've gotten a break, it begins to affect my moods, my energy levels, and my ability to think clearly and act decisively.*

In Chapter 4 I mentioned exercise as my main "stress buster," and for me, "stress buster" number two is solitude. Solitude allows me to reconnect with my soul, and it helps me to listen to my deepest yearnings. The "noise" and confusion of my everyday world can be left behind and I can just listen to what my soul is saying.

Being surrounded by the beauty of nature is my favorite way to find solitude. In nature I open my senses and soak in every moment. Many times as I stroll and breathe deeply I can feel the tension and the stress leaving my body. I'll look to the heavens and thank God for all of nature's miracles . . . the blazing colors of a fall hillside, the sound of a whippoorwill, or the breathtaking beauty of a sunset across the water.

I highly recommend setting aside pockets of time during each day for solitude. You might have only five or ten minutes, but be alone and uninterrupted. And then sometime each week devote an extended time—at least one hour—to reconnect with your soul. How and when you do it is a very personal thing, but plan it because solitude doesn't happen on its own. Make it a priority in your life.

Solitude is as needed to the imagination

as society is wholesome to the character.

JAMES RUSSELL LOWELL

WORK IS NOT ALWAYS REQUIRED OF A MAN.

THERE IS SUCH A THING AS A SACRED IDLENESS,

THE CULTIVATION OF WHICH IS NOW FEARFULLY NEGLECTED.

GEORGE MacDONALD

LIVE TODAY

SAVOR THE
Moment

I ONCE HEARD *someone say, "We don't remember days; we remember moments." However, at today's hectic pace we often forget to savor small pleasures while we make big plans.*

In the race to be better or best, we sometimes lose sight of "just being." And just being, just soaking in and savoring a beautiful moment, can provide some of life's greatest pleasures. A crackling fire on a cold winter night, a good book, a love letter from your spouse, a spectacular sunset, a great meal, or a timeless moment with your child or a friend . . . these moments, if we stop long enough to enjoy, are the essence of life.

I love to fish, especially for large–mouth bass. About three years ago I was watching television late one night and got this crazy notion to go fishing in the lake behind my house. Of course, my wife thought I was nuts. It was almost midnight! I convinced her I was sane and took off. I walked out to a warm summer breeze and looked up at the starry sky and breathtaking full moon. I allowed my senses to soak in every second—the sweet smell of honey suckle, the sound of every cricket and bullfrog, the moon's reflection dancing off the water—it was a perfect night. After walking across a small field, I took out a flashlight, and selected a lure. On my first cast I reeled in a bass weighing over five pounds, one of the largest I had ever caught. I gently released it back into the water and continued my midnight adventure. During the next two hours I caught seventeen bass, all between two and five pounds. Although I've fished for almost fifty years, no fishing memory can top that warm summer night.

But that night provided far more than a fishing memory. It was a life memory. It provided me a snapshot of what life could be like if I just slowed down enough to savor the moments. On my way back to the house, as I walked through the tall grass, I took one last look at the sky and stopped to say, "Thank You, God, for giving me this night."

We must not allow the clock

and the calendar

to blind us to the fact

that each moment is a miracle

and a mystery.

H. G. WELLS

SAVOR MOMENTS

TAKE ACTION

PROCRASTINATION
IS OPPORTUNITY'S
NATURAL
ASSASSIN.

Bridge the
GREATEST GAP IN LIFE

*Knowing is
not enough;
we must apply.
Willing is
not enough;
we must do.*

JOHANN
WOLFGANG
VON GOETHE

WOULD YOU LIKE *to take a guess as to what is the greatest gap in life? John Maxwell says the greatest gap is the one between* I should *and* I did. *It's commonly known as the procrastination gap, and we're all guilty at times.*

For example, about seven years ago I was in a Successories® store and watched a couple in their early forties stroll through the front door. The husband stopped, looked around for about thirty seconds, then nudged his wife and said, "Honey, these guys stole my idea! Remember when I said to you, 'I'll bet we could start a business selling products with motivational quotes.' Remember that?"

I smiled and when they left I shared the story with our store manager. She said, "Mr. Anderson, we probably have one person a month come in and say the same thing." Then, out of curiosity, I spoke to some of the other managers and they reported similar exchanges.

Hundreds of people had the idea, but only one executed it. This is a great example of the gap between I should and I did.

Procrastination, in my opinion, is opportunity's natural assassin.

Here's a tip to help cure the procrastination problem. There's an old saying that goes: "If the first thing you do when you get up in the morning is eat a live frog, then nothing worse can happen to you for the rest of the day." I'd have to say that's a pretty safe assumption!

Brian Tracy in his book *Eat That Frog* says "your frog" should be the toughest task of the day, the one you're most likely to procrastinate on. Eating that frog or completing that task, he says, can give you energy and confidence that will provide momentum for the rest of the day. On the other hand, Tracy says, if you let it sit there on the plate staring back at you while you're doing less–significant "stuff," it can drift into your subconscious, drain your energy, and you won't even know it.

So here's your assignment for the next month: Look at your things–to–do list, circle the frog, and . . . I really don't have to say it again, but you get the picture.

FOCUS

OFTEN HE WHO
DOES TOO MUCH,
DOES TOO LITTLE.
ITALIAN PROVERB

DISCOVER THE POWER *of Focus*

"IF YOU CHASE TWO RABBITS BOTH WILL ESCAPE."

In eight words this Chinese proverb captures the essence of focus. In business and in life, there is a natural tendency to think, "more is better," but I have to tell you that most of the time the opposite is true. To accomplish "more" we need to focus on "less." It's really that simple: focusing on your priorities can be key to your success in business and in life.

At Successories® in 1997, I learned about the power of focus the hard way. I didn't focus—and I paid the price. Golf was the hot sport because Tiger Woods had just come on the scene. We decided to purchase a small catalog company called British Links, a leader in golf art and golf gifts. The logic was simple: (1) we understood the specialty catalog business and (2) we understood the wall décor/framing business. Successories® had become one of the largest framers in the country and half of the British Links' sales were from framed wall décor. Therefore, we could leverage our expertise and economies of scale to make it work. It looked absolutely great on paper! (There's a book in there somewhere . . . *927 Reasons Why Things Look Great On Paper, But Won't Work*. I know lots of friends who could help me write it.)

I won't bore you with the details of why this venture flopped, but within three years we sold the golf company for next to nothing. However, the most devastating part of the deal was not the money we lost from the sale of British Links, but the momentum we had lost growing Successories®, our core business.

In hindsight, I was an idiot! It was like Ray Kroc after opening twenty McDonald's locations saying . . . it's time to get into the pizza business. He didn't, of course. He kept his eye on hamburgers and fries and made McDonald's the largest restaurant chain in the world. Many other businesses—like Starbucks and FedEx—also focused their way to success.

But remember this: Focus is not a "business only" thing. Each person has only twenty–four hours per day, and how we spend those hours shows what's important in our lives. The question we must ask ourselves is . . . Are we focusing on what really matters?

*Keep your eye
on the ball
and your head
in the game*

FOCUS

CHALLENGES

BY FACING
OUR CHALLENGES
WE DISCOVER
OUR POTENTIAL.

Fail FORWARD

IT IS EMBLAZONED *on my brain forever. I simply refer to it as the "fall of '94."*

From 1990 to 1993 Successories® grew over one hundred percent each year. We were mailing more than ten million catalogs annually and had opened sixty retail stores. We were on a roll. The simple concept of "decorate your walls with great ideas" had taken off.

Then Murphy's Law hit us like a ton of bricks. Everything that could go wrong, did. In June, Jim Allison, our CFO, was diagnosed with brain cancer at 47 years old. I was devastated for Jim and his family, and because of Jim's illness, software and fulfillment projects critical to our holiday success were delayed.

69

As hard as we tried, we couldn't catch up. The rapid growth had outstripped the company's infrastructure and our ability to manage it. It was every entrepreneur's nightmare, and when the dust settled in February, we discovered that our losses were significant. I must admit that for a guy in the attitude business, mine was pretty lousy for a few weeks.

Help came from Hall of Fame linebacker Mike Singletary, who had joined our board of directors the previous year. He recognized the problem, walked into my office, and closed the door. He said, "Mac, I want you to listen very carefully to what I'm going to say. This is only a bump in the road, and there is no doubt in my mind that you can fix what's broken. We've grown over one hundred percent each year . . . and I'll guarantee you one thing—it didn't happen by accident."

As Mike continued to speak, I could feel the goose bumps. I could feel my spine begin to stiffen. I could feel the belief and the courage returning. It was a pivotal moment in my life.

What did I learn about Mac Anderson—and my team—from that failure? I decided my strengths were my people skills and my creative abilities, while my weaknesses, like many entrepreneurs, were in the

details—accounting and operations that were critical to success. I needed help in those areas. I needed people who had done it already, people who could rebuild our infrastructure to grow the business again.

It was a painful wake–up call. I had failed greatly . . . but from that failure came valuable lessons.

Failure is a big part of life, but it's how we react to failing that will determine our destiny. If we learn from it and move on, it can help to make us all we can be. If you fear it to the extent that you never take risks, you'll never grow.

TO LIVE

There once was a very
*   cautious man,*
Who never laughed or cried,
He never cared, he never dared,
He never dreamed or tried.
And when one day he
*   passed away,*
His insurance was denied.
For since he never really lived,
They claimed he never died.

AUTHOR UNKNOWN

71

TO GET WHAT
YOU'VE NEVER HAD,
YOU MUST DO WHAT
YOU'VE NEVER DONE.

DISCIPLINE

Discover the Power
OF DISCIPLINE

ARISTOTLE SAID, *"We are what we repeatedly do. Excellence then is not an act but a habit." How true that is! If we make good habits, they invariably make us.*

In the fall of 1996 I received a phone call from an unforgettable young man. He introduced himself as Matt Ghaffari, and went onto tell me that a few months earlier he had won the silver medal in Greco–Roman wrestling during the 1996 Summer Olympics. He said he wanted to stop by while he was in Chicago, and I said, "No problem. I'd like to meet you."

A few hours later my receptionist called saying my guest had arrived. I walked to the lobby and there he was . . . 6'4" tall and 286 pounds of solid muscle. He had a huge smile on his face as we walked back to my office.

When we sat down, he said, "Mr. Anderson, I've come to thank you because you and your company have made a difference in my life." Then he reached into his left pocket and pulled out a green felt cloth, which he then opened. And there it was, his silver medal. It was beautiful! Then he reached into his right pocket and emptied the contents onto my desk. Amid his change was one of the brass medallions that we had created at Successories® with the words "Expect To Win."

He said, "Mr. Anderson, I've had that medallion in my pocket every day for three years. For the past four years I've worked ten hours a day, six days a week to train my body to be an Olympic champion. But I knew the difference in winning and losing was not going to be training my body; it was going to be training my mind to think positive, powerful thoughts . . . to believe I could do it. And the products you've created at Successories® have helped me to think like a champion."

You see, winners like Matt Ghaffari are never complacent. That is why they're winners. They understand the power of discipline. They understand one of my favorite laws in life—you cannot get what you've never had unless you're willing to do what you've never done.

Are you willing to make the sacrifices required to make your dreams come true?

*The difference between a successful person
and others is not a lack of strength,
not a lack of knowledge,
but rather a lack of will.*

DISCIPLINE

VINCE LOMBARDI

PATIENCE

THE TWO MOST
POWERFUL WARRIORS
ARE PATIENCE
AND TIME.

LEO TOLSTOY

LEARN WHEN TO *Wait*

I'LL BE THE FIRST TO ADMIT *that patience has not been one of my best virtues. However, as I've grown older, and hopefully wiser, I've come to appreciate its incredible power. In hindsight, I see that some of the major mistakes I made could have been avoided had I been more patient.*

In 1984, shortly after I sold McCord Travel, we started a small publishing company called Great Quotations. Our format was simple— each of our thirty titles had eighty pages with a single quote on the page. Our primary market was to hotel and airport gift shops.

The concept "took off" and within a year we had sold about a million books . . . but there was a problem. Because of the book's size and type of binding, none of the regional printing companies could do the job cost effectively. We had a choice: (1) we could source the book overseas where hand labor was inexpensive, or (2) we could purchase printing and custom collating equipment to do the work in-house.

I was impatient and decided to buy the equipment. Well, it was one of the worst business decisions I have ever made. Two years, and a million dollars later, we closed the printing operation, sold the equipment, and found an overseas source that did the job for half the price, with none of the headaches.

Fast is not always best. Had I been more patient and done a little more homework, I would have avoided the headaches and heartaches of going through the "learning curve."

Recently, I had a speaking engagement in Hawaii. I arrived about midnight and a driver met me at the airport to take me to my hotel. He was a young man with a real passion for life. On the way to the hotel, he shared his love for surfing. I asked him if it was dangerous and he said, "Very dangerous, if you don't know what you're doing." He said that many people drown when a large wave takes them under and their instincts tell them to fight to get back to the surface. The key, he said, is to do just the opposite; let your body go limp and the currents will bring you to the surface.

This can also be a life lesson. When you face adversity, be focused but patient, and the right answers will usually surface before you know it.

Patience is bitter,

but the fruit is sweet.

PATIENCE

EXERCISE

EXERCISE IS A

SMALL PRICE TO PAY

FOR A HEALTHY BODY

AND A HEALTHY ATTITUDE

EXERCISE TO *Energize*

A strong body makes the mind strong.

THOMAS JEFFERSON

ALTHOUGH IN AN EARLIER *chapter I mentioned exercise as one of the keys to managing my attitude, exercise merits its own chapter. I must admit that I was a slow learner to the physical and mental benefits of regular exercise . . . and I emphasize the word regular.*

For years, I had business friends who were fervent about working out three or four times a week, but I couldn't understand where they found the time. In hindsight I was a fool for not making the time, too. After exercise became a priority in my life, I found that my creativity, stress levels, energy, problem–solving abilities, and attitude were all impacted in a positive way. It has been an amazing discovery, and I can only hope that some of you will learn from my mistake and make it part of your life sooner than I did.

So what happens to your brain and your body when you exercise? During exercise the heart pumps more blood, which carries increased amounts of oxygen and nutrients to your cells, resulting in higher energy levels. The increased heart rate also causes blood to move through our arteries at a faster pace. Just as heavy rains wash "crud" from the sides of streams, rapid blood flow helps remove plaque from the artery walls.

A few months ago I was talking with a friend who is 65 years old but who looks ten years younger. I said, "Tony, you look great! How do you do it?"

He said, "I work two jobs!"

"What are you talking about?" I asked, knowing that he made a good living in his importing business.

He said, "My business is still going strong, but my other job is 6–7 a.m., five days a week on the treadmill. Once I started looking at it as a second job, I just did it whether I felt like it or not. In this case I don't get any financial gain, but what I get in physical and mental gains is priceless."

This was a great analogy, and since then when I feel less motivated to exercise, I think . . . second job, no excuses, get busy. Don't underestimate the benefits of regular exercise. Thirty to forty–five minutes a day, three to four times a week is a small price to pay for a healthy body and a healthy mind.

DIVERSITY

BEAUTY COMES IN ALL COLORS.

RECOGNIZE OPPORTUNITY
in Diversity

One world—

we're all in

this together.

I WAS SWEATING. *Dr. Moss was about to give us the final exam in freshman English.*

He told us our task was to write a theme presenting the merits of integrating schools. These were difficult times. Dr. Martin Luther King, Jr. had recently been killed, the National Guard had been called out in Mississippi to block James Meredith from entering Ole Miss. The nation was torn . . . especially in the South.

Of the thirty people in my class, twenty–nine were white and one was black. Much to my amazement, about five minutes into the two–hour exam the black student walked to the desk, handed Dr. Moss his paper, and left. I was shocked and thought maybe he was upset about the topic and was walking out in protest. However, I continued writing, and just before the two–hour mark turned in my paper.

Two days later the class gathered to receive their final grades, and all the themes were returned, except one. Dr. Moss said there were some good papers and there were some lousy papers. (I was thrilled with my B+.) But he said the one A+ was earned by Robert, the young black student in the first row. Dr. Moss said, "I'd like to read it to the class. It's short, and won't take long. In fact, it's only one sentence . . . fourteen words to be exact."

"It takes both the black and white keys to play
the Star Spangled Banner."

Wow! I remember the chills that went up my spine when I heard those words. What insight from this young man!

We are all in this world together. And think about it for a moment . . . if we were all totally committed to the Golden Rule, regardless of looks, religion, or skin color . . . can you imagine what a wonderful world it could be?

KINDNESS

NO ACT OF KINDNESS,

NO MATTER HOW SMALL,

IS EVER WASTED.

AESOP

Discover the Power
OF KINDNESS

The best portion of a good man's life, his little, nameless, unremembered acts of kindness and love.

WILLIAM WORDSWORTH

RALPH WALDO EMERSON *said, "One of the greatest compensations in life is that no person can help another without helping themselves." How true it is!*

Mary Kay Ash was the inspirational founder of Mary Kay Cosmetics. Many years ago I heard her speak to a group of executives, and she told of her first sales job when she was in her early 20s. She had been excited because she was attending her first convention, and was going to get to meet the top sales person of the company. At a reception, she made her way through the crowd, introduced herself, and asked the man to please share some of his secrets to success. And, do you know what he said . . . nothing. Absolutely nothing! He just walked away.

Mary Kay said it was a defining moment in her life, and she promised herself that if she ever enjoyed any success in her life, she would share it with others. Once she started her own company, she said, when she walked into a room she would pretend that everyone had a sign around their neck that said . . . MAKE ME FEEL IMPORTANT.

We all want to feel important, and one of the simplest acts of kindness, one of the simplest ways to make anyone feel important is to sincerely listen to what they have to say.

In my opinion, there is no real success, in any life, until they can discover the beauty of simple, random acts of kindness.

LISTEN

THE GREATEST GIFT
YOU CAN GIVE ANOTHER
IS THE PURITY
OF YOUR ATTENTION.

RICHARD MOSS

PERFECT THE
Art of Listening

*Remember not only
to say the right thing
in the right place,
but to leave unsaid
the wrong thing at
the tempting moment.*

BEN FRANKLIN

WHEN I WAS A SENIOR *in high school, I occasionally substitute–taught a Sunday School class for five–year–old boys. One Sunday, I was teaching twenty very active boys—do you know any that age who aren't?—a lesson on the Apostle Peter.*

During a little review I asked, "Who in the class would like to tell me who Peter was?" Dead silence. Not one hand went up. Then I said, "We've talked about this for twenty minutes, so surely someone knows the answer." With that a little boy with red hair said, "I t'ink Pet'a was a wabbit." It was an unforgettable moment.

We all know kids aren't the greatest listeners in the world, but that changes as we grow older and wiser, right? For many, I don't think so.

Without question, the art of listening is one of the most underestimated keys to success. I want you to stop and think about the friends you really enjoy being with, the bosses you've enjoyed working for, and I'd be willing to bet they all have one thing in common . . . they are good listeners.

A few years ago a friend called. He was distraught. He was going through some difficult times in his life, and was being forced to make some tough choices. We agreed to meet at a restaurant for lunch. We sat for over three hours, and he poured his heart out. Every fifteen minutes or so I'd ask a question and he would respond. At the end of his conversation, I could see the twinkle in his eyes, and the bounce was back in his step. He thanked me over and over again for sharing my advice. But you know what . . . I really offered no advice. In the three hours that we met, I'd estimate that he spoke for two hours and fifty-five minutes. But by my encouraging him to talk through his stressful situation, he was able to reach his own conclusions. The next day, he called and said, "Mac, I just figured out why I like you so much—when I'm with you, I feel good about me."

We all want to be heard. We all want to feel what we have to say is important, and you can convey no greater honor than to sincerely listen to what someone has to say.

PRIORITIES

> A HUNDRED YEARS FROM NOW, IT WILL NOT MATTER WHAT MY BANK ACCOUNT WAS, THE SORT OF HOUSE I LIVED IN, OR THE KIND OF CAR I DROVE ... BUT THE WORLD MAY BE DIFFERENT BECAUSE I WAS IMPORTANT IN THE LIFE OF A CHILD.

PUT FIRST THINGS *First*

I MET CHARLIE CULLEN *through his nephew during my sophomore year in college. Charlie had been ranked by his peers as the top speaker in the country, and he had addressed the leaders of many Fortune 500 companies. But on this day, as a favor to his nephew, he interrupted his schedule to address a small group of students on the Keys to Success. For almost an hour, he spoke passionately about courage, humility, perseverance, and believing in your dreams. And he ended with a story I never forgot.*

He said that he was in the Oklahoma City airport when he saw a woman walking along with three little girls. They were skipping and singing, "Daddy's coming home on a big jet! Daddy's coming home on a big jet!" All excited! Eyes lit up like diamonds! Wild anticipation! They had never before met Daddy coming home on a jet. Their mother was so proud of them and their enthusiasm. You could see it in her eyes.

Then the plane arrived, the door opened and the passengers streamed in. You didn't have to ask which one was Daddy. The girls' bright eyes were glued on him. But his first look was for his wife. Spying her, he yelled, "Why didn't you bring my top coat?" and strode right past his adoring, crushed daughters.

Here was a man who had an opportunity to be great, and he didn't recognize it.

How many times a day, a week, a month do we have the opportunity to be great, and not even know it?

Of all the beautiful lithographs that we've created at Successories®, everyone seems to remember one in particular. It is the photo of a small boy looking out at the ocean. The title is *Priorities*, and it says:

> "A hundred years from now it will not matter what my bank account was,
> the sort of house I lived in, or the kind of car I drove . . .
> But the world may be different because I was important in the life of a child."

These words truly bring the meaning of "real success" into focus.

PRIORITIES

*The main thing is
to keep the main thing,
the main thing.*

INTEGRITY

A QUIET CONSCIENCE
SLEEPS IN THUNDER.

ENGLISH PROVERB

Be True to Your CONVICTIONS

It is no use walking anywhere to preach unless our walking is our preaching

ST. FRANCIS
OF ASSISI

"YOUR TRUE CHARACTER *is revealed by the clarity of your convictions, the choices you make, and the promises you keep. Hold strongly to your principles and refuse to follow the currents of convenience."* This great quote, on a Successories print, is one of my favorites on Character. With every decision you make, you are shaping the person you will become. Choosing right over wrong, truth over popularity . . . these are the choices that will measure your life.

Ken Duncan is one of the best panoramic photographers in the world. I spent two days with Ken and his wife, Pam, at their home just north of Sydney, Australia. While I was there Ken shared the story of some of the adversity he experienced while publishing his beautiful coffee table book, *America Wide.*

He wanted to create a book that would capture the diversity and splendor of America in all fifty states. The monumental project consumed much of his time and resources for two years.

He had negotiated a contract with a major publisher, but they disagreed on what the cover of the book should say. Ken is a spiritual person and wanted the cover to read *America Wide* with a lightly screened subtitle saying, *In God We Trust.* The publisher, however, refused to reference God on the cover. Ken had to make an extremely difficult decision. Would he take the safe route and agree with the publisher who had worldwide distribution, or would he self–publish the book that had taken over two years to create? He chose to follow his convictions to keep the *In God We Trust* on the cover. Although the financial risk was great, compromising his belief was unacceptable.

He made the right choice . . . *America Wide* has been a great success and has sold more than 250,000 copies.

John Wooden, the great basketball coach, said it well, "Adversity does not build character . . . it reveals it."

EXCELLENCE

EXCELLENCE IS NOT AN ACT,

IT IS A HABIT.

ARISTOTLE

COMMITTED TO *Excellence*

Countless unseen details are often the only difference between mediocre and magnificent.

ONE OF MY FAVORITE QUOTES *is this one from Vince Lombardi, legendary coach of the Green Bay Packers: "The quality of a person's life is in direct proportion to their commitment to excellence, regardless of their chosen field of endeavor."*

The people for whom I have the most respect are those who make sacrifices to become all they can be. God gives each of us unique talents, and maximizing those talents is one of life's challenges. Whether you are a mother, a mechanic, a business person, whatever . . . your goal should be to make the most of those God-given talents, to heed the "inner voice" that inspires you to learn and grow.

After more than thirty years in business, I have come to realize that a common denominator for every successful person I've known is what I'll call the "and then some" ingredient. No one attains greatness simply by doing what is required; it is what they do beyond the required that takes them to the pinnacle.

Michael McKee, the senior vice president of creative for Successories®, fits the "and then some" definition perfectly. Michael's unwavering commitment to quality and excellence has been critical in building the Successories® brand. Many times since we started the company in 1988 we've had to tighten our belts to survive downturns in the economy, but we never, ever sacrificed the quality of the product by cutting corners. Quality has always been the "mother" of our business, and we don't mess with Mom.

A quote on one of our lithographs captures the essence of Michael McKee's commitment to excellence: "Countless, unseen details are often the only difference between mediocre and magnificent."

Stand out from the crowd. Be the "and then some" person in your business, your family, and in all you do.

PERSEVERE

ANYONE CAN HOLD
THE HELM ·
WHEN THE SEA
IS CALM.

Persevere!

IF SOMEONE WERE TO ASK ME *to pick one word to describe any success I've enjoyed, I wouldn't hesitate: the word would be "perseverance."*

In the past thirty years I've been involved in three startup companies—Orval Kent, McCord Travel, and Successories®—and I'm pleased to say they all became leaders in their niches. However, none of them succeeded without what I would call a "near death" experience. Many times along the way I had people on the sidelines saying, "Mac, it's time to quit. Throw in the towel, it's over." I'm glad I didn't listen.

My assistant, Marj Webber, knows how I feel about perseverance, and recently she came into my office and said, "You're going to like this one." With that she handed me a story titled "Shake It Off and Step Up." After you read it, I think you'll understand why the parable about an old mule has a special place in my heart.

Shake It Off and Step Up

A farmer owned an old mule that fell into a well.
After assessing the situation, the farmer reluctantly concluded that neither the mule nor the well was worth saving. Instead, he called his neighbors together and enlisted them to help bury the old mule in the well and put him out of his misery.

Initially the old mule was frantic, but as the dirt kept hitting his back, something happened. It dawned on the mule that every time a shovel load landed on his back, he should SHAKE IT OFF AND STEP UP! This he did, blow after blow. Shake it off and step up . . . shake it off and step up. No matter how painful the blows or how distressing the situation, the old mule fought panic and just kept right on SHAKING IT OFF AND STEPPING UP!

Before long, the old mule, battered and exhausted, stepped triumphantly through the mouth of that well. What seemed like it would bury him, actually helped him . . . all because of how he handled his adversity.

Such is life. If we face our problems and respond to them positively, refusing to surrender to panic, bitterness, or self–pity, the adversities that come along to bury us usually possess the potential to benefit us.

Nothing in the world can take the place of persistence.
Talent will not; nothing is more common
than unsuccessful men with talent.
Genius will not; unrewarded genius is almost a proverb.
Education will not; the world is full of educated derelicts.
Persistence and determination alone are omnipotent.

CALVIN COOLIDGE

RISK

TO STRIVE,
TO SEEK,
TO FIND,
AND NOT TO YIELD.

ALFRED LORD TENNYSON

BEWARE THE PATH OF
Least Resistance

ALMOST THREE YEARS AGO, *I was in my office awaiting a very important call. My heart was pounding and my mouth was dry. When the phone rang, the voice on the other end told me what I hadn't wanted to hear. I had Prostate Cancer. My life would never be the same. What had been important in my "world of business" immediately became insignificant. My new focus was to ask God to help me make the right decisions about my treatment and about what to do with the rest of my life.*

I had been in entrepreneurial businesses for thirty years, and I decided to remove myself from the day-to-day pressures of running a company. I was 54 years old and was ready to "smell more roses" by golfing, fishing, and traveling with my family.

However, after my treatment and then a year of relaxing, I realized that I wasn't ready to retire. So, in addition to consulting for Successories®, I decided to look for another challenge that would be fun, but flexible enough to allow free time.

Before my illness, I had enjoyed speaking to various companies and universities, but I'd been limited in the amount of time I could commit to it. After my illness, however, I did have the time, but I questioned whether I really wanted to make the travel commitment.

My deliberation came to a head when I heard Lee Ann Womack singing her hit song, *I Hope you Dance.* I turned the radio up and soaked in the beautiful words that helped me to get off the path of least resistance. At some point all of us need a nudge to do what we know is right, and the words of this song about embracing life provided exactly what I needed.

How many of us go through life with unrealized dreams because we're afraid to take a risk? Think about what gives your life meaning—it's not the things you are given, it's what you achieve.

I'm pleased to say that my cancer is in remission and for the last few years I've truly loved sharing what I've learned about business and about life with many corporate audiences around the country.

As the song says,

> *When you get the choice to sit it out or dance*
> *I hope you dance . . . I hope you dance.*

I chose to dance . . . and hope you will, too.

It's easier to go down the mountain than up,
but the view from top is best.

SUCCESS

LOVE &
Be Loved

I RECENTLY HAD DINNER *with someone who told me that one of his best friends had been killed in a private plane crash, and something happened at the service that he'll never forget. He shared the story with me.*

At the memorial service his friend's wife walked to the podium to speak to the gathering. She said a friend had asked her the best memory she had of their life together. At the moment, she had been too grief–stricken to answer, but she had thought about it since and wanted to answer the question.

They were in their late forties when he died, and she began talking about a time in their life almost twenty years earlier. She had quit her job to obtain her master's degree, and her husband never wavered in his support.

BELOVED, LET US

LOVE ONE ANOTHER,

FOR LOVE IS OF GOD;

AND EVERYONE

WHO LOVES

IS BORN OF GOD

AND KNOWS GOD.

1 JOHN 4:7, NKJV

He held down his own job and also did the cooking, cleaning, and other household chores while she studied for her degree.

One time they both stayed up all night. She was finishing her thesis, and he was preparing for an important business meeting. That morning she walked out on their loft, looked at him over the railing, and just thought about how much she loved him. She knew how important this meeting was to his career, and she was feeling guilty that she didn't even have time to make his breakfast. He grabbed his briefcase and hurried out. She heard the garage door open and close, but much to her surprise, she heard it open again about thirty seconds later. From above, she watched her husband dash into the house and walk over to the neglected coffee table. Tracing his finger through the dust, he wrote the words, "I love you." Then he raced back to his car.

The new widow then looked out at her audience and said, "John and I had a wonderful life together. We have been around the world several times, we've had everything money can buy . . . but nothing comes close to that moment."

Life moves with lightning speed. It feels like yesterday that I graduated from college . . . and now thirty–five years have passed. Although I'm very proud of my business accomplishments, in the end my life comes back to two things: my relationships and my faith in God.

You learn to speak by speaking,

to study by studying,

to run by running,

to work by working;

in just the same way,

you learn to love by loving.

ST. FRANCIS DE SALES

I WILL LIE DOWN AND SLEEP IN PEACE,
FOR YOU ALONE, O LORD,
MAKE ME DWELL IN SAFETY.

PSALM 4:8, NIV

PLACE YOUR
Faith in God

IN THE END, THE TRUEST MEASURE *of success is where you spend eternity. What kind of house you've lived in and what kind of car you've driven will mean nothing. But what will matter are these . . . how many hearts you've touched and whether you've placed your trust in God.*

It has become so easy to get caught up in life's pace in the pursuit of "stuff" and take things for granted—until a day like September 11, 2001, comes along. It stops us cold. It makes us realize every day is a wonderful gift from God, and how we use that day will help shape our destiny. Sir Francis Bacon said, "We have only this moment—sparkling like a star in our hand and melting like a snowflake."

Since that tragic September day I, like most of you, have done some soul-searching, and I've come to realize that I need God's guidance, love, and wisdom more than ever. Just last weekend I was driving back from

Wisconsin with my wife, and we saw a sign in front of a small church that really puts things in perspective. It said, "People who think they'll be saved at the 11th hour often die at 10:30." Oh how true it is! Life is fragile. We're only on this earth for a brief moment against the backdrop of eternity.

In business, and in life, we continually are faced with difficult choices. We draw from our experience, our instincts, and the advice of others whom we respect. But for me the best answers can come from asking one simple question: What would Jesus do? That question, combined with prayer, can produce powerful results.

Prayer is the link between us and God. We are never alone when He is in our lives. Consider the words of the old hymn *What A Friend We Have in Jesus*:

> Oh, what peace we often forfeit.
> Oh, what needless pain we bear,
> All because we do not carry
> Everything to God in prayer.

How true that is! In our most difficult times prayer can flood our soul with peace. Just knowing, always knowing, that we don't have to fight the battle alone can give us the courage, the clarity, and the peace of mind to fight on.

I will lie down and sleep in peace, for You alone, O LORD, make me dwell in safety (PSALM 4:8, NIV).

My personal thanks to Ken Jenkins and Todd Reed, who are not only great nature photographers, but also great human beings.—Mac

KEN JENKINS IS A NATIONALLY known naturalist, outdoor writer, publisher, lecturer and natural history photographer whose articles and photographs have appeared in more than 300 national publications. His lectures and workshop program (Sponsored by Nikon, Inc. for four years) have carried him throughout the National Park System and into major cities in the Southeast. Ken makes his home in Gatlinburg, Tennessee, where he owns and operates several galleries. Ken's photos appear on the back cover and on pages: 8, 16, 24, 32, 34, 36, 38, 47, 59, 60, 64, 76, 84, 86, 88, 99, 102, 115, 119, 122.

For more information, please visit www.kenjenkins.com.

GREAT LAKES BEAUTY AND POWER have dominated Todd Reed's photographs for more than thirty years. Todd's book, *Ludington: Point to Point,* captures the magnificence of Lake Michigan waters and adjacent lands near his Ludington, Michigan home. The award-winning photographer's life is focused on four passions: family, outdoor photography, teaching photography, and operating rescue boats in the Coast Guard Reserve. Todd's photos appear on pages: 4, 28, 40, 44, 50, 55, 56, 79, 80, 91, 100, 116.

For more information, please visit www.toddreedphoto.com.

MAC ANDERSON is the Founder of Successories, Inc, the leader in designing and marketing products for motivation and recognition. Successories, however, is not the first success story for Mac Anderson. He was also the Founder, and CEO of McCord Travel the largest travel company in the Midwest, and Part Owner/VP of Sales and Marketing for Orval Kent Food Company, the country's largest manufacturer of prepared salads. Mac's accomplishments in these three unrelated industries provide some insight into his passion and leadership skills.

Mac brings the same passion and conviction to his speaking engagements. "These 30 years of blood, sweat and tears as an entrepreneur have taught me a lot about business and about life that I love sharing with others," Mac says. Mac speaks on a variety of topics, including inspiration, leadership, motivation, and team building. For more information, please visit www.macanderson.com.